T0402793

SPORTS SUPERSTARS

JUAN SOTO

BY THOMAS K. ADAMSON

TORQUE™

BELLWETHER MEDIA · MINNEAPOLIS, MN

Torque brims with excitement perfect for thrill-seekers of all kinds. Discover daring survival skills, explore uncharted worlds, and marvel at mighty engines and extreme sports. In *Torque* books, anything can happen. Are you ready?

This edition first published in 2023 by Bellwether Media, Inc.

No part of this publication may be reproduced in whole or in part without written permission of the publisher. For information regarding permission, write to Bellwether Media, Inc., Attention: Permissions Department, 6012 Blue Circle Drive, Minnetonka, MN 55343.

Library of Congress Cataloging-in-Publication Data

LC record for Juan Soto available at: https://lccn.loc.gov/2022050046

Editor: Kieran Downs   Designer: Josh Brink

Printed in the United States of America, North Mankato, MN.

TABLE OF CONTENTS

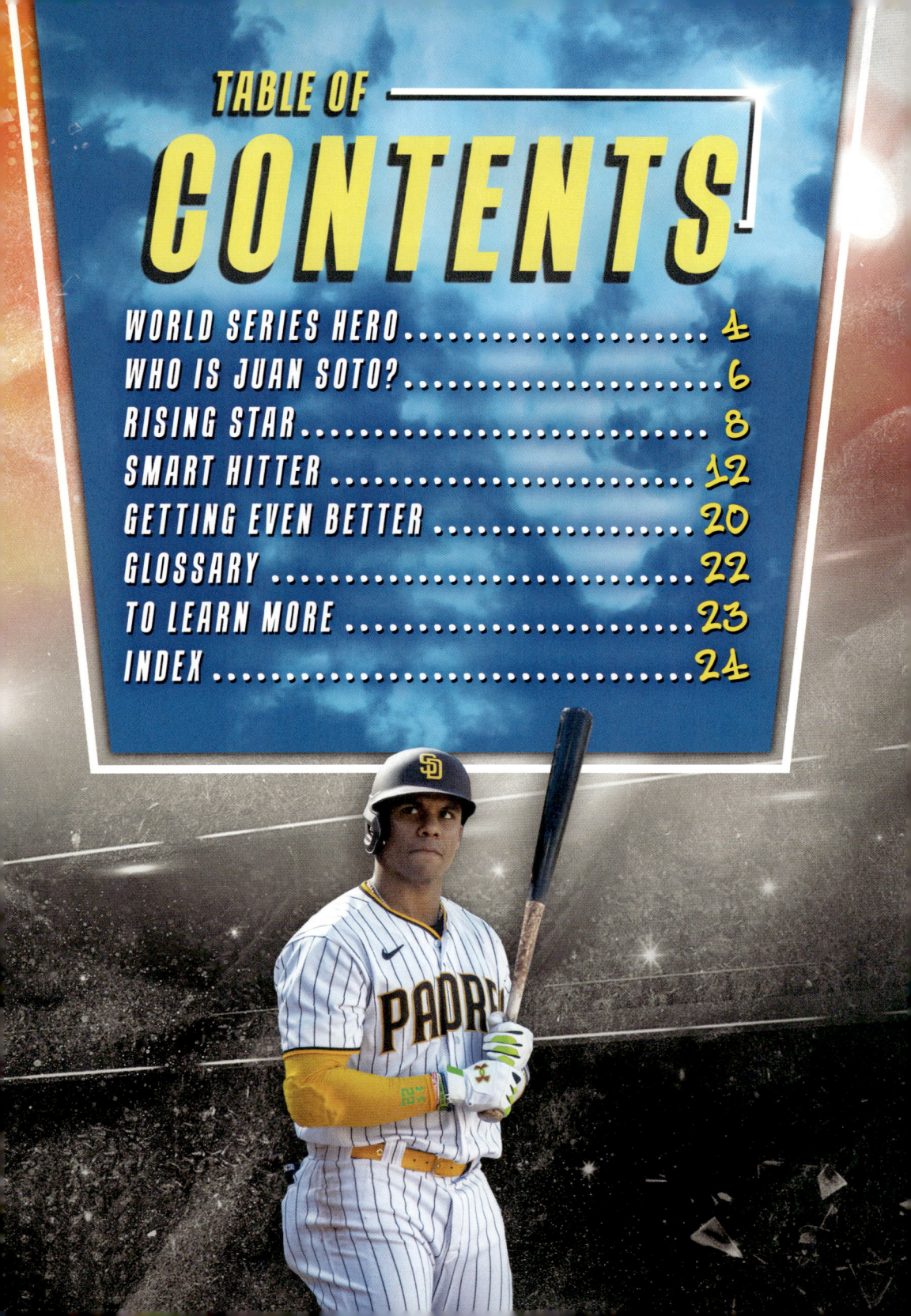

WORLD SERIES HERO

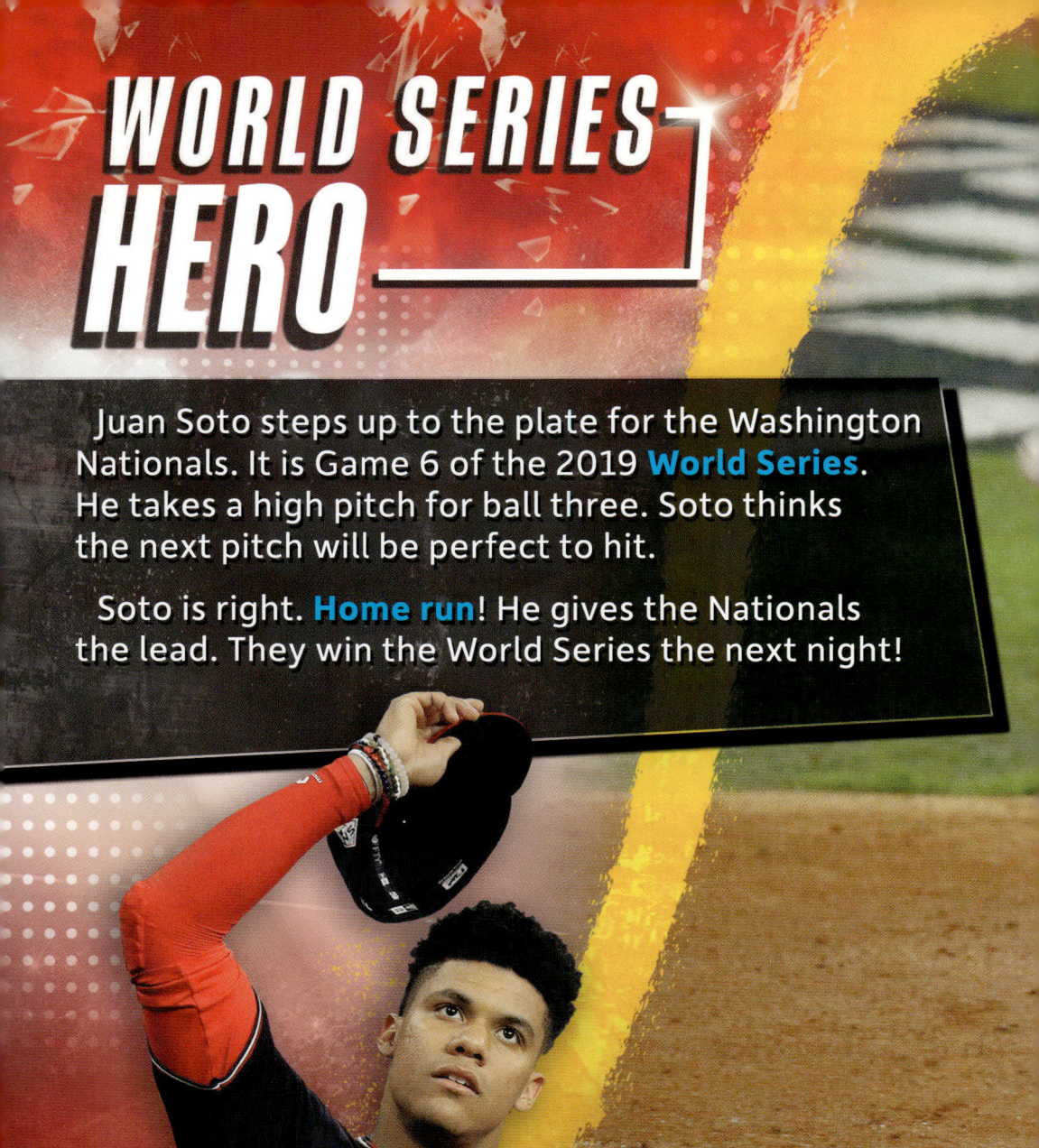

Juan Soto steps up to the plate for the Washington Nationals. It is Game 6 of the 2019 **World Series**. He takes a high pitch for ball three. Soto thinks the next pitch will be perfect to hit.

Soto is right. **Home run**! He gives the Nationals the lead. They win the World Series the next night!

4

Young Home Run Hitter

Soto hit a home run in Game 1 of the 2019 World Series. He became the fourth player younger than 21 years old to hit a home run in the World Seres.

5

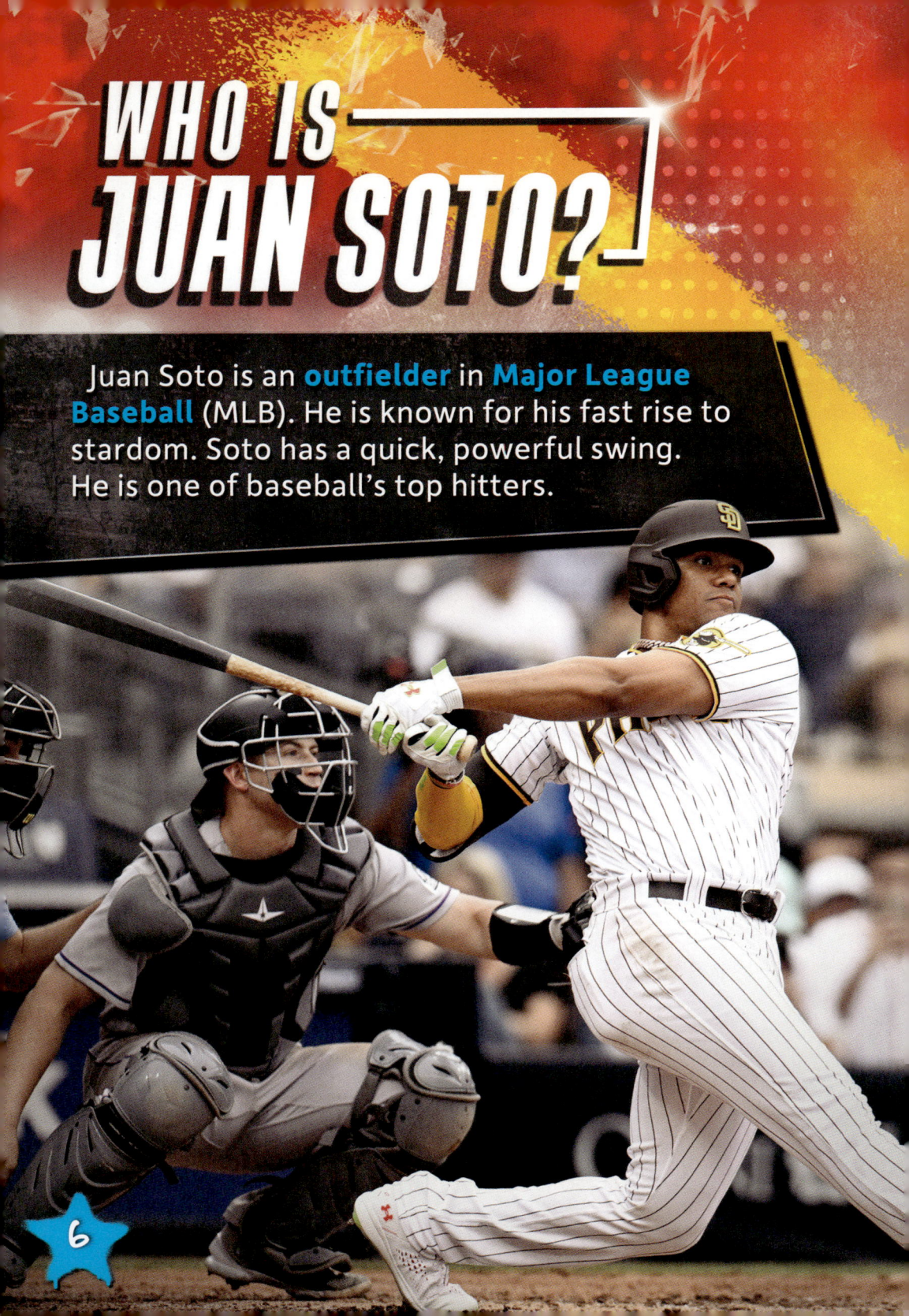

WHO IS JUAN SOTO?

Juan Soto is an **outfielder** in **Major League Baseball** (MLB). He is known for his fast rise to stardom. Soto has a quick, powerful swing. He is one of baseball's top hitters.

JUAN SOTO

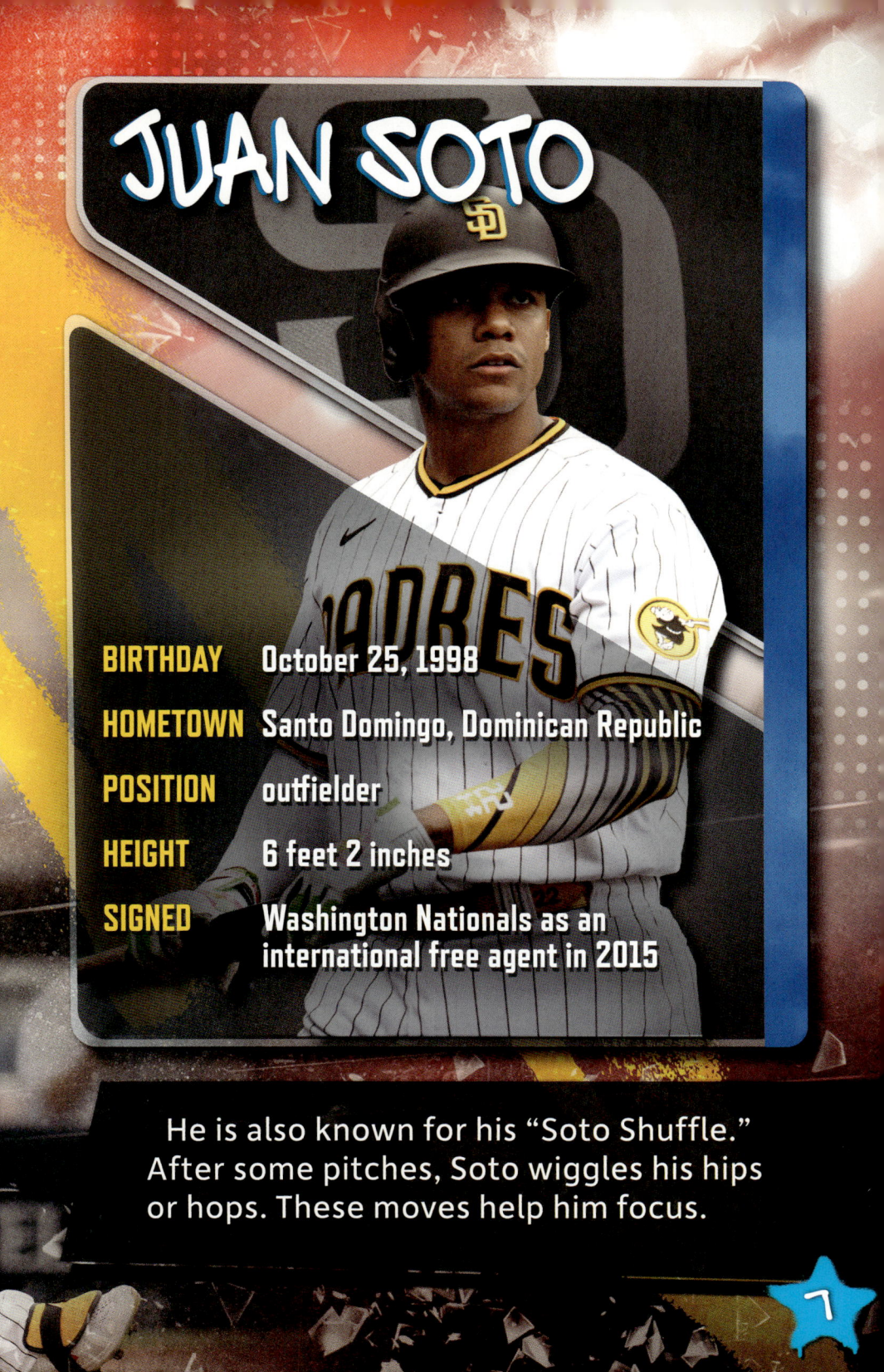

BIRTHDAY	October 25, 1998
HOMETOWN	Santo Domingo, Dominican Republic
POSITION	outfielder
HEIGHT	6 feet 2 inches
SIGNED	Washington Nationals as an international free agent in 2015

He is also known for his "Soto Shuffle." After some pitches, Soto wiggles his hips or hops. These moves help him focus.

7

RISING STAR

Soto loved baseball as a kid. He pretended to play baseball in his home with a crumpled-up piece of paper.

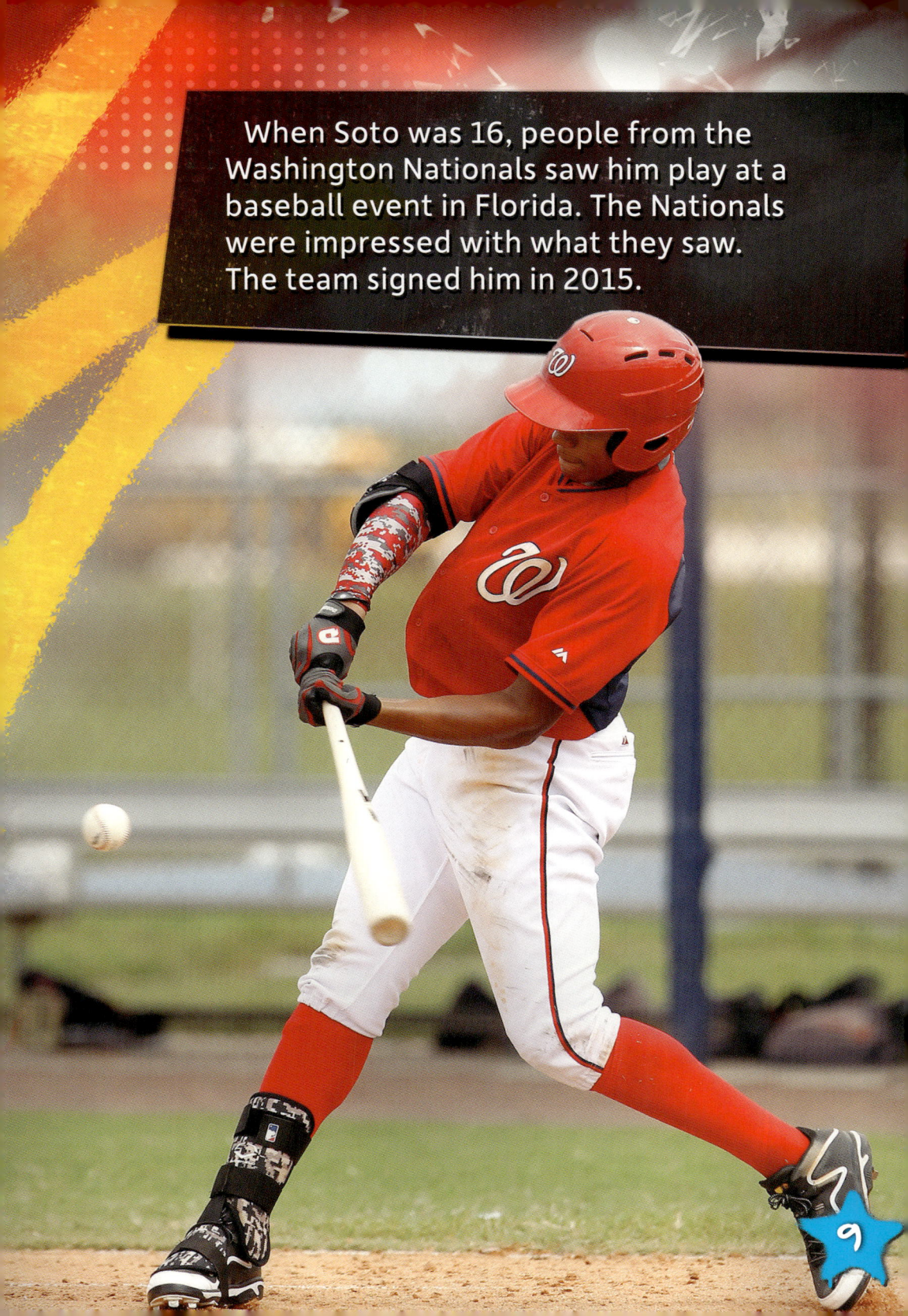

When Soto was 16, people from the Washington Nationals saw him play at a baseball event in Florida. The Nationals were impressed with what they saw. The team signed him in 2015.

9

Soto proved he was a great player in the **minor leagues**. In his first year, he was named **Most Valuable Player** (MVP) of the league he played in.

Soto quickly moved up through the minor leagues. He joined the Nationals major league team in May 2018. He was only 19 years old.

FAVORITES

DRINK
juice

FOOD
pastelón de plátano maduro

OTHER SPORT
basketball

PLAYER
Robinson Canó

11

SMART HITTER

Soto wasted no time showing he was already a great hitter. In 2018, he was one of the top first-year players in MLB.

Early Big Hits

Soto hit a three-run home run his second time batting in the major leagues!

12

Soto showed his star power in the 2019 World Series. In Game 1, he got three hits. Soto hit three home runs during the series. He helped the Nationals win their first World Series!

2019 WORLD SERIES WINNERS

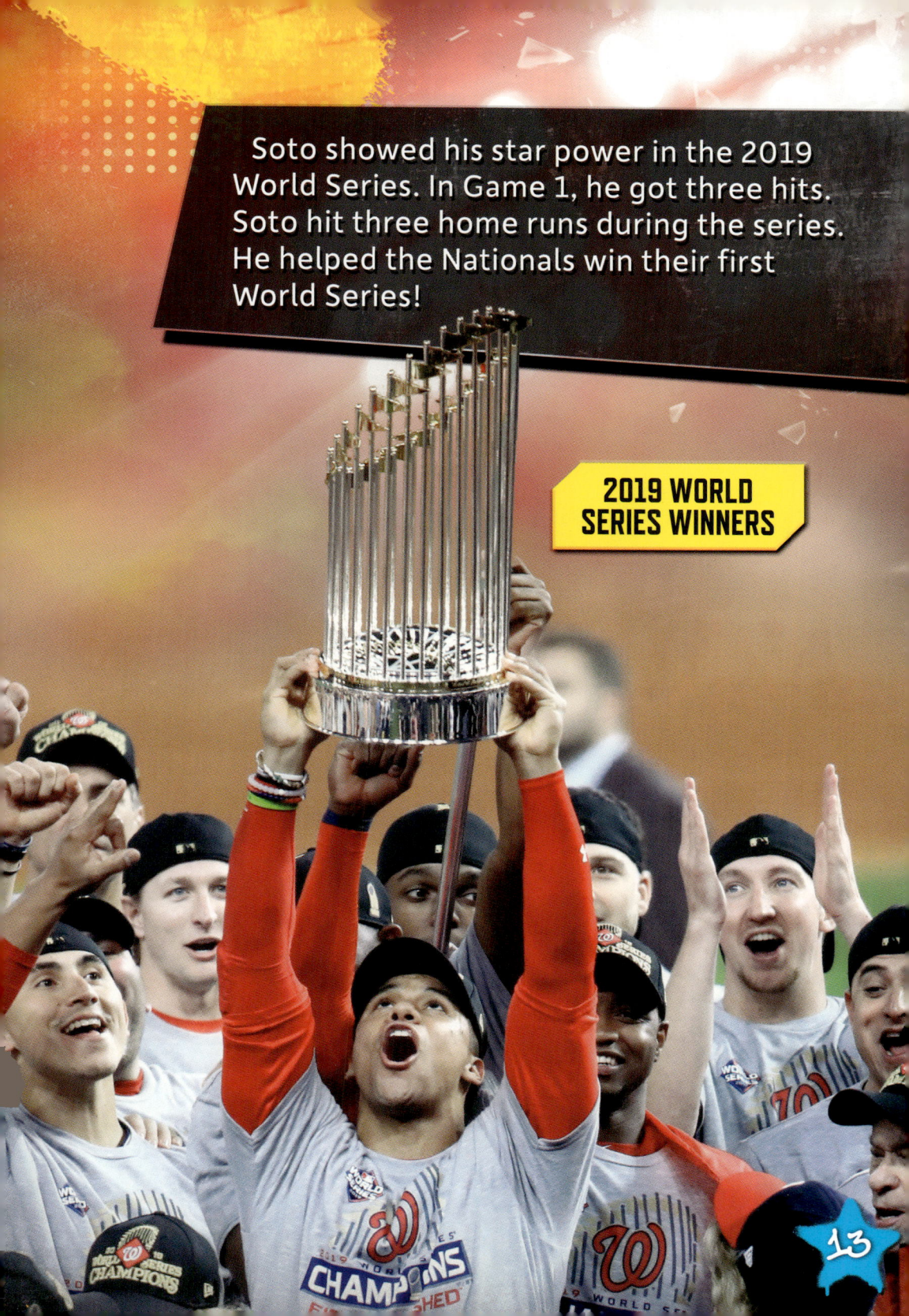

13

Soto kept hitting well after the World Series. In 2020, Soto won the **National League** (NL) batting title.

Counting both hits and **walks**, Soto reached base in almost half of his at bats in 2020. Soto also hit 13 home runs. He won his first **Silver Slugger** Award.

JUAN SOTO MAP

- ◎ **Washington Nationals, Washington, D.C.** 2018 to 2022
- ◎ **San Diego Padres, San Diego, California** 2022 to present

2020 SILVER SLUGGER

15

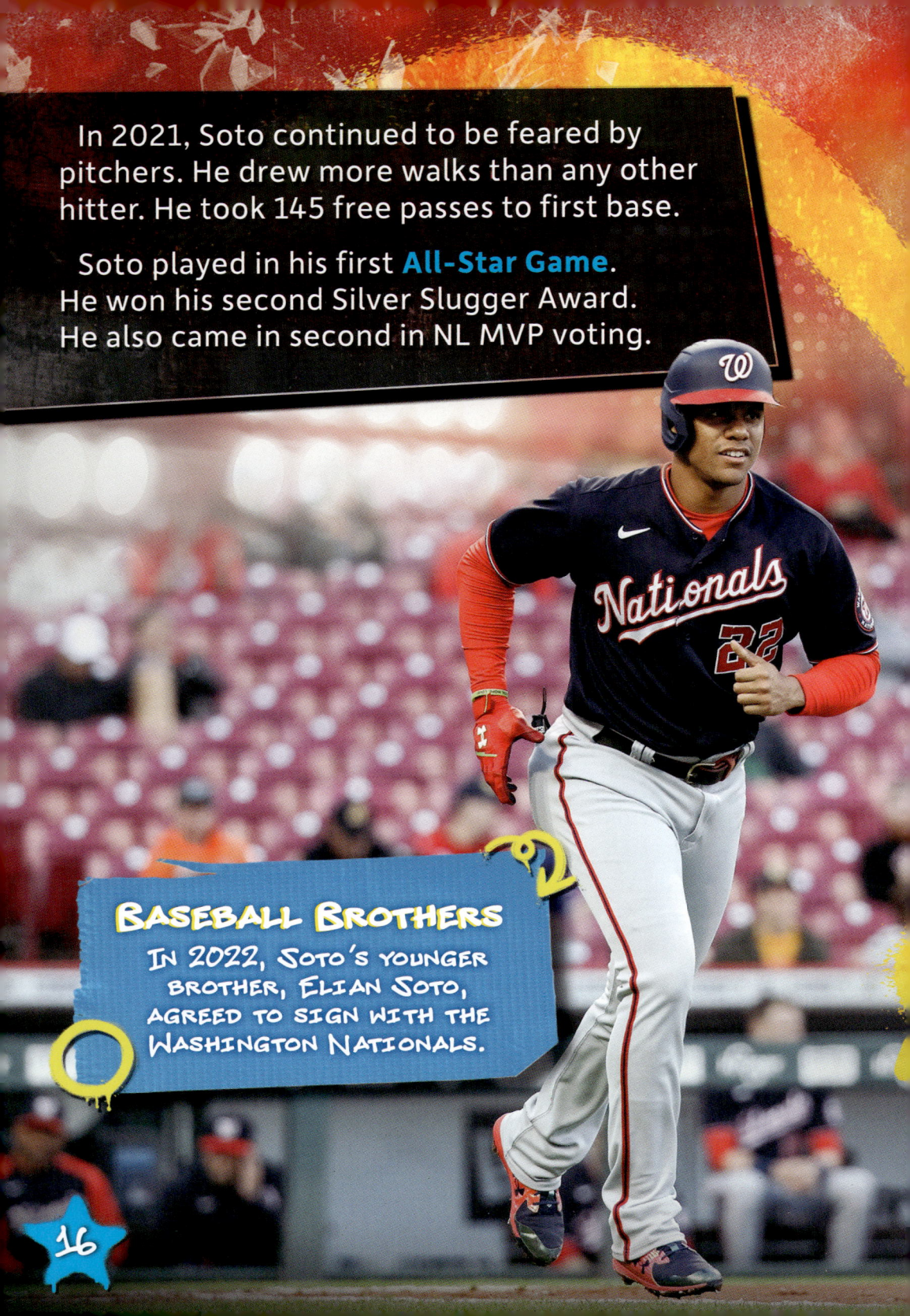

In 2021, Soto continued to be feared by pitchers. He drew more walks than any other hitter. He took 145 free passes to first base.

Soto played in his first **All-Star Game**. He won his second Silver Slugger Award. He also came in second in NL MVP voting.

BASEBALL BROTHERS

IN 2022, SOTO'S YOUNGER BROTHER, ELIAN SOTO, AGREED TO SIGN WITH THE WASHINGTON NATIONALS.

2021 SILVER SLUGGER

TROPHY SHELF

World Series champion

NL batting champion

Gulf Coast League MVP

2-time Silver Slugger

17

Soto was a solid hitter in 2022. He continued to lead MLB in walks. In April, he hit his 100th Major League home run. He was named to his second All-Star Game.

In August, Soto was traded to the San Diego Padres. He helped the team make it to the **playoffs**!

TIMELINE

— 2020 —

**Soto wins the
NL batting title**

— 2021 —

**Soto plays in his
first All-Star Game**

— 2022 —

**Soto is
traded to the
San Diego Padres**

GETTING EVEN BETTER

Juan Soto became a great hitter at a young age. He says he is still working on improving. That should make opposing pitchers nervous! He wants to keep collecting batting awards.

20

Soto hopes to be a star player for many more years. He has a bright future ahead of him!

21

GLOSSARY

All-Star Game—a game between the best players in a league

home run—a hit where the batter runs all the way around the bases and scores a run

Major League Baseball—a professional baseball league in the United States; Major League Baseball is often called MLB.

minor leagues—professional baseball leagues below Major League Baseball

most valuable player—the best player in a year, game, or series; the most valuable player is often called the MVP.

National League—one of the two large groupings of teams in Major League Baseball; the other is the American League.

outfielder—a position in baseball in which a player stands far away from the batter to catch hit balls

playoffs—games played after the regular season is over; playoff games determine which teams play in the championship game.

Silver Slugger—an award recognizing the best hitter of each position in baseball

walks—when hitters go to first base after pitchers throw four pitches that are not strikes

World Series—the championship series in Major League Baseball, played between the best team in the American League and the best team in the National League

TO LEARN MORE

AT THE LIBRARY

Berglund, Bruce. *Baseball GOATs: The Greatest Athletes of All Time*. North Mankato, Minn.: Capstone Press, 2022.

Hill, Christina. *Juan Soto*. Minneapolis, Minn.: Lerner Publications, 2022.

Martin, Andrew. *Baseball's Greatest Players: 10 Baseball Biographies for New Readers*. Oakland, Calif.: Rockridge Press, 2022.

ON THE WEB

FACTSURFER

Factsurfer.com gives you a safe, fun way to find more information.

1. Go to www.factsurfer.com

2. Enter "Juan Soto" into the search box and click 🔍.

3. Select your book cover to see a list of related content.

INDEX